WAKE UP
&
WATER SKI

KIMBERLY P. ROBINSON

BRISTOL FASHION PUBLICATIONS, INC.
Rockledge, Florida

WAKE UP & WATER SKI

Published by Bristol Fashion Publications, Inc.

ISBN: 1-892216-33-7
LCCN: 00-133182

Contribution acknowledgments

Cover Design: John P. Kaufman
Cover & Interior Art: Sue K. Pine

DEDICATION

For my mother Sue, who with her great illustrations made this book complete. And for my family, Eric, Ashley, and Logan, thank you for all your love and support.

WAKE UP & WATER SKI

WAKE UP & WATER SKI

It is a bright summer morning when young Logan wakes up at his house on the lake. Logan is so excited, because today is a special day! Today is the day his dad is going to teach him to water ski.

WAKE UP & WATER SKI

Logan is so excited he can hardly wait! He jumps out of bed, puts on his swimsuit and runs into the kitchen.

WAKE UP & WATER SKI

"Well, good morning Logan", says Dad from the kitchen table. "Are you ready to learn to ski today?" "I sure am!" replies Logan. "Good." smiles Dad, "Let's finish up in here and head for the dock."

WAKE UP & WATER SKI

After breakfast, Logan and Dad walk through the back yard toward the dock. Dad had already asked neighbor Steve to meet them at the dock. Steve is going to ride with them in the boat and help Dad watch Logan ski. This is called a spotter.

WAKE UP & WATER SKI

Their shiny red ski boat is tied to the dock. Dad helps Logan strap on his life vest. Together with Steve, they walk down the dock and climb into the shiny ski boat.

WAKE UP & WATER SKI

Dad starts the engine, unties the boat from the dock, and steers it onto the open water. The boat speeds through the water. Logan smiles because he loves the way the wind feels against his face when he rides in the boat.

WAKE UP & WATER SKI

Soon they come to a big open space in the water. Dad stops the boat and turns off the engine. "OK, Logan. This is it. Are you ready to learn to ski?" asks Dad.
"I sure am!" replies Logan.

WAKE UP & WATER SKI

Dad picks up the water skis and together, he and Logan climb onto the platform at the back of the boat. With their feet dangling in the water, Logan and Dad sit on the wooden platform. Dad helps Logan put on the two small wooden skis. Because they are training skis, they are tied together at the tips with a thick cord. This helps the skier control the skis.

WAKE UP & WATER SKI

Dad slides Logan into the water and away from the boat. He tosses Logan the handle to the ski rope that is attached to the back of the boat. Logan wobbles from side to side in the water trying to control the skis. "Relax, son." Dad says. "Just pull your knees to your chest, point the tip of your skis up and keep your arms straight."

"OK, dad", replies Logan.

WAKE UP & WATER SKI

Dad starts the engine of the boat. "I'm going to tighten up the ski rope now", Dad yells. "When you're ready to go, yell 'hit it!'" Dad puts the boat in gear and it slowly moves forward. Logan can feel the rope begin to tighten and tug in his hands.

WAKE UP & WATER SKI

With a scared look on his face, Logan yells, "Hit it!" When he does, Dad pushes down on the throttle of the boat. The boat speeds up and Logan stands straight up on the water. With a quick jerk, Logan pulls his arms in towards his chest and falls back in the water. "You have to keep your arms straight, son!" yells Dad

"I know," said Logan. "I want to try again!"

WAKE UP & WATER SKI

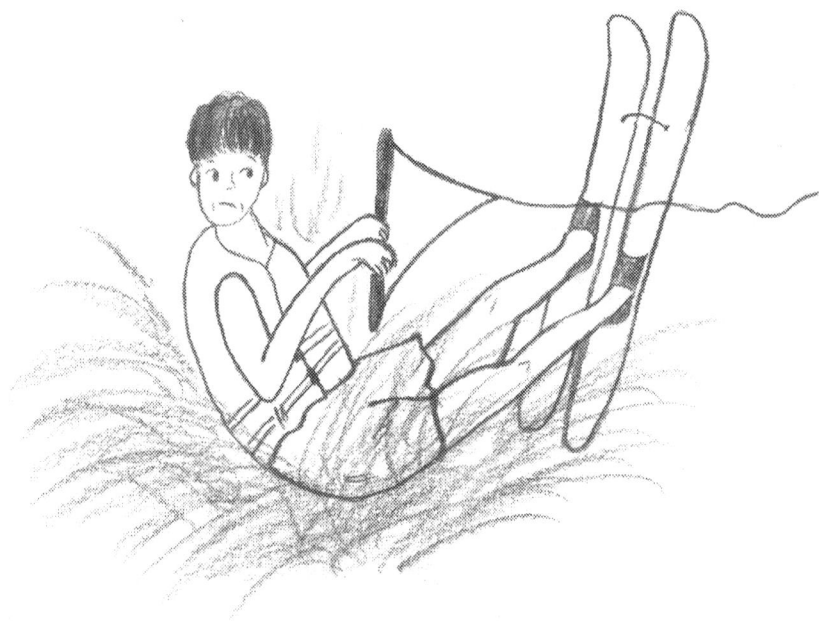

Logan tries to water ski several more times. Sometimes he falls backwards. Sometimes he falls to the side. Each time he falls, he learns something new about the right way to get up on water skis. The last time Logan yells "Hit it!" he stands up on his skis, but this time he does not fall. With his arms straight in front of him, his knees slightly bent, and a big smile on his face, he is water skiing! Dad is so excited he yells and screams with joy.

WAKE UP & WATER SKI

After Logan finishes water skiing, he climbs back into the boat. "I'm so proud of you!" Dad says as he gives Logan a big hug.

With a big grin on his face, Logan says, "Yeah, I'm pretty proud of me, too!"

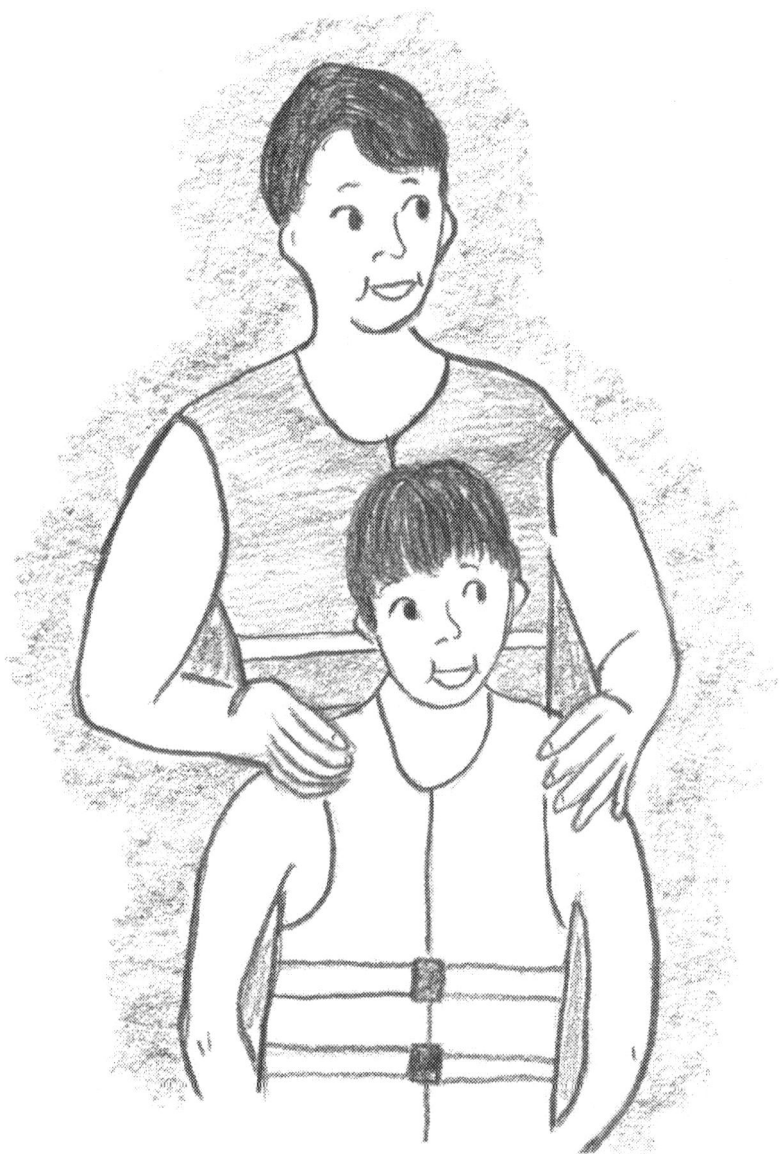

WAKE UP & WATER SKI

Drawing Fun!

On the following pages, see if you can draw some fun pictures about a day spent on the water!

WAKE UP & WATER SKI

WAKE UP & WATER SKI

Draw a picture of a boat that you could see while water skiing.

WAKE UP & WATER SKI

Draw a pair of beautiful water skis that have lots of colorful decorations.

WAKE UP & WATER SKI

While water skiing, you might see dolphins! Draw some friendly dolphins.

WAKE UP & WATER SKI

What other animals might you see from the ski boat? Draw them here.

WAKE UP & WATER SKI

WAKE UP & WATER SKI

WAKE UP & WATER SKI

Children's Books from
Bristol Fashion Publications
www.wescottcovepublishing.com

Wake Up & Water Ski
By Kimberly P. Robinson

My Grandpa is a Tugboat Captain
By Ken Kreisler

Billy the Oysterman
By Ken Kreisler

Daddy & I Go Boating
By Ken Kreisler

WAKE UP & WATER SKI

ABOUT THE AUTHOR

Since the age of 10, I have spent most of my summer weekends boating on the lakes of North Carolina and Virginia. It was on Kerr Lake in Virginia that I met the man that I would later marry. After marriage and a week before the birth of our first child, we purchased our first new inboard/outboard boat. Several years later, we purchased a new Mastercraft Ski Boat.

As a family, we participate in various water sports including slalom skiing, barefoot skiing, knee boarding, wake boarding, and my five-year old son's favorite, tubing! We still own the Mastercraft along with a summer home on Kerr Lake in Virginia. It is there that I now spend much of the summer since retiring my position as a Corporate Tax Accountant. I now dedicate most of my time to writing, particularly children's books, and to my family.

WAKE UP & WATER SKI

www.ingramcontent.com/pod-product-compliance
Lightning Source LLC
Chambersburg PA
CBHW031530040426
42445CB00009B/466